D0109079

Pirandello's Henry IV

Plays
Rosencrantz and Guildenstern Are Dead ★
Enter a Free Man ★ • *The Real Inspector Hound* ★
After Magritte ★ • *Jumpers* ★ • *Travesties* ★
Dirty Linen and New-Found-Land ★
Every Good Boy Deserves Favour ★
Night and Day • *Dogg's Hamlet and Cahoot's Macbeth* ★
The Real Thing • *Rough Crossing* • *Hapgood*
Arcadia • *Indian Ink* • *The Invention of Love* ★
Voyage: The Coast of Utopia Part I ★
Shipwreck: The Coast of Utopia Part II ★
Salvage: The Coast of Utopia Part III ★

Television Scripts
A Separate Peace • *Teeth* • *Another Moon Called Earth*
Neutral Ground • *Professional Foul* • *Squaring the Circle*

Radio Plays
The Dissolution of Dominic Boot
"M" Is for Moon Among Other Things
If You're Glad, I'll Be Frank • *Albert's Bridge*
Where Are They Now? • *Artist Descending a Staircase*
The Dog It Was That Died • *In the Native State*

Screenplays
Rosencrantz and Guildenstern Are Dead
Shakespeare in Love (with Marc Norman)

Fiction
Lord Malquist and Mr. Moon

★Available from Grove Press

Pirandello's Henry IV

BY LUIGI PIRANDELLO

A NEW VERSION BY TOM STOPPARD

Grove Press
New York

Printed in the United States of America

FIRST EDITION

Library of Congress Cataloging-in-Publication Data
Stoppard, Tom.
 Pirandello's Henry IV / by Luigi Pirandello ; a new version by Tom Stoppard.— 1st ed.
  p. cm.
 ISBN 0-8021-4194-3
  1. Henry IV, Holy Roman Emperor, 1050–1106—Drama. 2. Psychotherapist and patient—Drama. 3. Aristocracy (Social class)—Drama. 4. Italy—Drama. I. Title: Pirandello's Henry the Fourth. II. Stoppard, Tom. III. Pirandello, Luigi, 1867–1936. Enrico IV. English. V. Title.
 PR6069.T6P57 2005
 822'.914—dc22   2004063842

Grove Press
an imprint of Grove/Atlantic, Inc
841 Broadway
New York, NY 10003

05 06 07 08 09 10 9 8 7 6 5 4 3 2 1

ACKNOWLEDGMENTS

This version was prepared with the help of a literal translation by Francesca Albini, commissioned by the Donmar Theatre, and with further assistance from Simonetta Wenkert. I take sole responsibility for the departures from Pirandello.

Tom Stoppard's new version of *Henry IV* by Luigi Pirandello was commissioned by and first performed at the Donmar Warehouse, London, on April 29, 2004. Michael Grandage, artistic director; Nick Frankfort, executive producer; Tobias Round, general manager. The cast was as follows:

HENRY IV   Ian McDiarmid

LANDOLF   James Lance

HAROLD   Stuart Burt

ORDULF   Neil McDermott

BERTOLD   Nitzan Sharron

GIOVANNI   Brian Poyser

DI NOLLI   Orlando Wells

BELCREDI   David Yelland

DOCTOR   Robert Demeger

MATILDA   Francesca Annis

FRIDA   Tania Emery

It was directed by Michael Grandage; the designer was Christopher Oram; the lighting design was by Neil Austin; the music and sound score was by Adam Cork; and the sound designer was Fergus O'Hare.

Pirandello's Henry IV

ACT ONE

The throne room. There are two full-length, life-size modern portraits of a young man and a young woman dressed as Henry IV and Matilda, Countess of Tuscany. HAROLD, LANDOLF, ORDULF, *and* BERTOLD—*wearing the costumes of eleventh-century German knights—enter.*

LANDOLF Next—the throne room!

HAROLD The throne room of the Emperor's Palace at Goslar!

ORDULF Or could be Hartzburg . . .

HAROLD . . . or Worms, depending.

LANDOLF Depending on where we are in the story—he keeps us on the hop.

ORDULF Saxony . . .

HAROLD Lombardy . . .

LANDOLF The Rhine . . .

ORDULF Keep your voice down.

LANDOLF He's asleep.

BERTOLD Hang about. I'm confused. I thought we were doing *Henry IV*.

LANDOLF So?

BERTOLD Well, this place, these getups—it's not him.

ORDULF Who?

BERTOLD The King of France, Henry IV.

LANDOLF Whoops.

ORDULF   He thought it was the French one.

LANDOLF   Wrong country, mate, wrong century, wrong Henry.

HAROLD   It's the German Henry IV, Salian Dynasty.

ORDULF   The Holy Roman Emperor.

LANDOLF   The Canossa one—walked to Canossa to get absolution from the Pope. Church v. State, that's the game round here, day in, day out.

ORDULF   Emperor at home to Pope—

HAROLD   Pope away to Anti-Pope—

LANDOLF   King away to Anti-King—

ORDULF   Like war with Saxony—

HAROLD   Plus with revolting barons—

LANDOLF   His own kids . . .

BERTOLD   Now I know why I've been feeling wrong in these clothes; these are not your French 1580s.

HAROLD   Forget the 1580s.

ORDULF   Think the ten hundreds.

LANDOLF   Work it out; if Canossa was January 1077 . . .

BERTOLD   I'm fucked.

ORDULF   Royally.

BERTOLD   I've been reading up the wrong . . .

LANDOLF   Sad. We're four hundred years behind you. Ahead of you. You're not even a twinkle in our eye.

BERTOLD (*angered*)   You got any idea how much stuff I read in the last two weeks about Henry IV of France?

HAROLD   Didn't you know Tony was our Adalbert, Bishop of Bremen?

BERTOLD   What Adalbert?—no one told me anything!

LANDOLF   Well, when Tony died, at first the young Count . . .

BERTOLD   The Count Di Nolli? He's the one who gave me the job. Why didn't he . . . ?

ORDULF   He must have thought you knew.

LANDOLF   . . . first he thought the three of us would do. Then Himself started moaning—"They've driven out Adalbert!"—he didn't realise "Adalbert" had died on us, he thought the bishops of Cologne and Mainz had booted him out, Tony I mean—all clear so far?

BERTOLD   Wait. Bishop Tony of what?

ORDULF   You're fucked.

HAROLD   Forget the bishops. The bishops are not the problem, the problem is we don't know who you are.

BERTOLD   So what am I playing?

ORDULF   Um, Bertold.

BERTOLD   Bertold who? Why Bertold?

LANDOLF   Himself kept yelling, "They've driven out Adalbert, so get me Bertold! I want Bertold!"

HAROLD   We eyeballed each other—who dat?

LANDOLF   Never heard of him.

ORDULF   And here you are.

3

LANDOLF   You'll be great.

BERTOLD   No, I won't, which way's out?

HAROLD   No, no, relax.

LANDOLF   This'll cheer you up—we don't know who we are either. He's Harold, he's Ordulf, I'm Landolf, that's what he calls us so that's who we are, you get used to it, but it's a puppet show. Who are we really? . . . Just names of the period. Same with you, I suppose, Bertold. Tony was the only one with a proper character, the Bishop of Bremen. He was a good bishop, too, God rest him.

HAROLD   Always reading himself up.

LANDOLF   And he bossed Himself about, not himself, Himself, His Majesty; he was like his teacher. With us, we're his Privy Counsellors but we're only here to take up space. It's in the books—the barons had it in for Henry for surrounding himself with young bloods not quite premier league, so that's us. Royal hangers-on, do anything for him, like a drink, a few laughs . . .

BERTOLD   Laughs?

HAROLD   Just do what we do.

ORDULF   It's not as easy as it looks.

LANDOLF   Bit of a waste really. We've got the scenery, we've got the costumes, we could put on proper shows, history's always popular, and there's enough stuff in *Henry IV* for several tragedies. But us four—we're stranded, nobody gives us our moves, nothing to act, it's that old form-without-content. We're worse off than the real ones. They were given sod-all to play, true, but they didn't know that, so they just did what they did because that's what they did.

4

Life. Which means, look after number one. They sold titles and stuff. And here we are, great outfits, handsome surroundings, shame about the puppets.

HAROLD No, fair do's, you have to be ready to come out with the right answer or you're in trouble.

LANDOLF Yeah, that's true.

BERTOLD Well, that's it, innit? How'm I supposed to give him the right answer when I've been learning the wrong Henry?

HAROLD You'll have to put that right right off.

ORDULF We'll all pitch in.

HAROLD There's lots of stuff on him, a quick skim will do you for now.
(*indicating portrait*) Here's one . . . who's the skirt, do you know?

BERTOLD Her? Well, spot the deliberate mistake . . . she doesn't belong, for a start, a modern picture like that . . .

HAROLD You're not wrong, you're right.

LANDOLF But here's the thing—it's only a mistake if you think of them as portraits.

BERTOLD Which is what they are.

LANDOLF They are and they aren't. To Himself, seeing as he never touches them—

BERTOLD So what are they to him?

LANDOLF This is just my theory but I bet I'm right—to him they're more like representations of—what you'd see in a mirror. That one is him just as he is, same clothes, in this

5

throne room, which is right in every detail, no surprises. If it was a mirror, you'd see yourself in the eleventh century. So that's what *he* sees. Himself. So it's like mirrors reflecting back a world which comes to life in them, like it will for you, you'll see, don't worry.

BERTOLD   Don't worry?

HAROLD   It's a laugh.

BERTOLD   So how did you get to be so into it . . . ?

LANDOLF   Over nine hundred years of experience.

ORDULF   Take your cue from us.

BERTOLD   What about her—the Emperor's wife?

HAROLD   Not at all. His wife is Bertha of Susa, sister of Amadeus II of Savoy.

ORDULF   He can't stand her. He wants to dump her. He likes being one of the lads, like us.

LANDOLF (*indicating portrait*)   That's his sworn enemy— Matilda, the Countess of Tuscany.

HAROLD   The one who put the Pope up.

LANDOLF   At Canossa.

ORDULF   Pope Gregory VII. We hate him. (*a bell tolls*) You're on. Go out there an unknown, come back a star. Let's go.

They brace themselves to go "onstage," move to exit, but GIOVANNI *enters, in modern dress.*

GIOVANNI (*hurried and anxious*)   Hey . . . psst—Franco! Lolo!

HAROLD   What's up?

BERTOLD   Hey. What's he doing here?

6

LANDOLF Wrong century—get out!

ORDULF Get thee hence!—emissary of Gregory VII!

HAROLD Be gone!

GIOVANNI Leave off!

ORDULF 'Tis forbidden!

HAROLD This be sorcery!

LANDOLF (*to Bertold*) A spirit conjured up by the Wizard of Rome! Quick, draw your sword.

GIOVANNI (*yelling*) Stop taking the piss. The young Count has arrived . . . with a party . . .

LANDOLF Ah! Great! Any women?

ORDULF Good-looking?

GIOVANNI There's two gentlemen.

HAROLD What about the women?

GIOVANNI The Countess and her daughter.

LANDOLF (*surprised*) Oh!—how come?

ORDULF The Countess?

GIOVANNI That's right—the Countess.

LANDOLF (*to Bertold*) Her daughter is engaged to the young Count.

HAROLD And the men?

GIOVANNI I don't know them.

HAROLD (*to Bertold*) A bit of content.

ORDULF Messengers from the Pope—this is more like it.

GIOVANNI Will you let me tell you?

HAROLD Go on, then.

GIOVANNI I think one's a doctor.

LANDOLF Oh, right, another doctor.

HAROLD (*to Bertold*) You brought us luck!

LANDOLF Watch us work the doctor.

BERTOLD I think I'm out of my depth.

GIOVANNI Listen—they want to come in.

LANDOLF Here? *She* can't come in here.

HAROLD Now that's what I'd call content.

LANDOLF We'd have a real tragedy on our hands.

BERTOLD Why's that?

ORDULF (*pointing at the portrait*) It's *her,* don't you see?

HAROLD What do they want in here?

ORDULF If Himself sees her he'll blow his lid.

LANDOLF That's if he still knows her.

GIOVANNI If he wakes up, you're to keep him out.

ORDULF Oh, easy!—and how're we supposed to do that?

GIOVANNI Bloody hell—use force if you have to. I've been told—get on with it.

HAROLD He could already be awake.

ORDULF Let's go.

LANDOLF Tell us later what's going on.

8

GIOVANNI Lock the door and take the key out.

Landolf, Harold, Ordulf, and Bertold leave. DI NOLLI *comes in.*

DI NOLLI All clear?

GIOVANNI Yes, my lord.

Di Nolli exits for a moment to invite the others in. The first to enter is BARON TITO BELCREDI, followed by DOCTOR DIONISIO GENONI, then COUNTESS MATILDA and her daughter FRIDA. Giovanni bows and exits. Matilda is about forty-five years old; she is still beautiful although she repairs the inevitable damage with heavy but expert makeup. Belcredi is lean, prematurely grizzled, slightly younger. Frida is only nineteen. She's already engaged to Count Carlo Di Nolli, a stiff young man in full mourning. They enter nervously, looking at the room with curiosity (except for Di Nolli) and almost whispering to begin with.

BELCREDI Incredible . . .

DOCTOR Fascinating! The dementia carried through to the last detail.

MATILDA Ah, there it is. Yes, yes . . . Look at it . . . My God . . . Frida, look . . .

FRIDA Oh, your portrait!

MATILDA No. Look. It's not me, it's you.

DI NOLLI What did I tell you?

MATILDA But it's uncanny! Look, Frida—can't you see it's you?

FRIDA Well . . . really I . . .

MATILDA Look, Tito.

BELCREDI Wouldn't dream of it, on principle.

9

MATILDA Idiot! He thinks he's being gall-ant. You tell her, Doctor.

BELCREDI *Psst*—Doctor—for pity's sake—don't get involved in this.

DOCTOR In what?

MATILDA Ignore him. He's insufferable.

FRIDA He plays the fool for his supper, didn't you know?

BELCREDI Watch where you're putting your feet!

DOCTOR Why?

BELCREDI Hobnailed boots.

DOCTOR Really?

BELCREDI And you're about to step on somebody's toes.

DOCTOR Oh . . . come on . . . what's so strange about a daughter looking like her mother?

BELCREDI Crunch, too late!

MATILDA Why, what did he say?

DOCTOR Nothing special.

BELCREDI He said there was nothing strange about it. In which case, why did you act so stunned?

MATILDA (*enraged*) For the very reason that the resemblance is so natural—fool!—because that's my portrait and to see my daughter looking back at me was an amazing thing, so I was amazed—all right?—and you can keep your insinuations to yourself.

Embarrassed silence.

FRIDA Oh God, it always ends in a row.

BELCREDI (*apologetically*) I wasn't insinuating anything. I just happened to notice you didn't share your mother's amazement. If you were surprised at anything, it was at your mother being amazed.

MATILDA Well, obviously! She didn't know me when I was her age. But I caught sight of myself and I saw I was . . . just like she is now.

DOCTOR No more than one would expect. Because for the daughter it's just a picture, a moment caught and complete in itself . . . while for the mother it comes with a whole string of associations—how she moved, gestured, smiled, spoke, everything which isn't in the portrait . . .

MATILDA Exactly.

DOCTOR . . . all sprung to life in your daughter.

MATILDA Thank you! But when I speak as I feel, he has to go and spoil it to annoy me.

DOCTOR (*continues in his professional tone, turning to Belcredi*) Resemblance, you see, my dear Baron, often resides where you least expect it—which is how . . .

BELCREDI Which is how some people might even find a resemblance between you and me.

DI NOLLI Please, please, we've got off the point.

FRIDA That's what happens when he's around.

MATILDA Which is exactly why I didn't want him to come.

BELCREDI How ungrateful, after all the fun you have at my expense.

DI NOLLI Tito, I beg you—enough. The Doctor is here, we have serious business, and you know how important this is to me.

DOCTOR Good. Let's make a start by getting a few things clear. How did this portrait come to be here? Did you give it to him back at the beginning?

MATILDA No, how would I? I was just a girl—like Frida—not even engaged. I let him have the picture three or four years after the accident because Carlo's mother wouldn't leave me alone about it.

DOCTOR (*to Di Nolli*) Your mother being his sister?

DI NOLLI Yes. We're here because we promised her. She died a month ago. But for that, Frida and I would be on our honeymoon.

DOCTOR With your mind on other things—I understand.

DI NOLLI Mother died convinced that her brother was about to get better.

DOCTOR And can you tell me why she thought so?

DI NOLLI It was a conversation they had not long before she died.

DOCTOR Did they now? It would be useful to know what he said.

DI NOLLI I wish I could help you. All I know is she came back obviously upset. I gathered he'd spoken to her with unusual tenderness, almost as if he knew it was the last time . . . and on her deathbed she made me promise not to abandon him, to have him seen . . .

DOCTOR And here we are. So first, let's see . . . sometimes the tiniest event can . . . This portrait, then . . .

12

MATILDA   Oh, heavens, we mustn't exaggerate its importance—it was just that I hadn't seen it for so long.

DOCTOR   Please . . . patience . . .

DI NOLLI   Well, quite—it's been there for about fifteen years.

MATILDA   Nearer eighteen.

DOCTOR   Please!—you don't know yet what I'm asking. In my belief these two portraits may be crucial. They were done, I suppose, before the famous—or should I say infamous—pageant, is that right?

MATILDA   Of course.

DOCTOR   When he was still in his right mind—that's the point I was making. Were they his idea?

MATILDA   No, not at all. Lots of us who took part decided to have our portraits done as a souvenir of the pageant.

BELCREDI   I had mine done—Charles of Anjou.

DOCTOR   You don't know if it was he who asked for it?

MATILDA   I've no idea. It's possible. Or it might have been Carlo's mother's idea of humouring him.

DOCTOR   Now, another thing. Was this pageant his idea?

BELCREDI   No, it was mine.

MATILDA   Don't take any notice of him. It was poor Belassi's idea.

BELCREDI   Belassi?

MATILDA   (*to the Doctor*)   Count Belassi, poor man, who died two or three months later.

BELCREDI But Belassi wasn't even there when I . . .

DI NOLLI Excuse me, Doctor, does it really matter whose idea . . .

DOCTOR It could be important.

BELCREDI It was mine! This is too much! Do you think I'd brag about it after what happened? You see, at the Club we'd been thinking of putting on a show for the next carnival. So I suggested this historical pageant, I say historical, it was more of a hodgepodge, everyone had to choose a character from this or that century, a king, or emperor, or prince, with his lady—queen or empress— beside him, also on horseback. The horses had all the period trappings, too, of course. That was my suggestion and it was adopted.

MATILDA Well, my invitation came from Belassi.

BELCREDI Theft. Belassi wasn't even in the Club that night. Nor was *he*.

DOCTOR So then he chose Henry?

MATILDA That's because, my name being Matilda, I said off the top of my head that I'd be Countess Matilda of Tuscany. He said, in that case he'd be Henry IV.

DOCTOR I'm sorry, I don't see the connection.

MATILDA I didn't either at first. He said he'd be at my feet just like at Canossa. I knew about Canossa but only vaguely, and when I looked it up I found I was the Pope's most zealous ally against the German King Henry. I blushed from top to toe. I understood why he'd chosen to be Henry IV.

DOCTOR You mean, perhaps, because . . .

14

BELCREDI Dear God, Doctor—because he was mad about her, and she couldn't stand him.

MATILDA That's not true! I didn't dislike him; quite the opposite. But whenever a man gets all serious about a woman—

BELCREDI He turns into a complete ass . . .

MATILDA No, he wasn't like you, my dear.

BELCREDI But I've never asked to be taken seriously.

MATILDA Don't we know it. But with him, you had to take him seriously back. (*to the Doctor*) Among the misfortunes we women have to put up with from time to time is suddenly being confronted by a pair of eyes gazing at us with the solemn promise of lifelong devotion. (*She bursts into laughter.*) There's nothing more ridiculous. If only men could see themselves doing their lifelong devotion look. It always made me laugh. More so in those days. But now, after twenty years, let me confess something. When I laughed at him, it was partly out of fear, because, coming from him, you felt he could mean it. And that would have been extremely dangerous.

DOCTOR Now this, this is something I want to know about. Extremely dangerous, you say?

MATILDA (*lightly*) Well, because he wasn't like the others . . . and I wasn't brave enough not to laugh it off . . . anyway I had no patience for anything serious, I was just a girl, I hadn't done my share of living, so I laughed along with everyone else. I was sorry later . . . I hated myself, actually, because my laughing at him got all mixed up with those fools laughing at him.

BELCREDI Like they do with me, more or less.

MATILDA   You make people laugh by humiliating yourself—that's the opposite.

DOCTOR   So, as I understand it, he was already in a bit of a state.

BELCREDI   Yes, but in his own way.

DOCTOR   What do you mean?

BELCREDI   Dispassionately in a state.

MATILDA   Dispassionately!? He threw himself into life—

BELCREDI   I'm not saying he was putting it on. Not at all. He was often worked up. But I'd swear he'd immediately dissociate himself from the state he was in, observing himself—even, in my view, when he was at his most spontaneous. I think, furthermore, it had a harmful effect on him. Sometimes he'd get into these hilarious fits of rage against himself.

MATILDA   That's true, he did.

BELCREDI   And why was that? (*to the Doctor*) The way I see it, that outside view of himself, like someone watching himself playing a part, separated him from what he was feeling—which then seemed to him not exactly fake, because he wasn't faking his feelings, but something he had to act out as a self-conscious intention, to make up for the authenticity he couldn't feel. So he would go to extremes, improvise, exaggerate, anything to lose his self-awareness . . . that's why he'd come across so erratic, frivolous, even at times ludicrous.

DOCTOR   And . . . antisocial, would you say?

BELCREDI   No, not at all! He was game for anything—he was famous for organising dances, tableaux vivants, benefits—all for the fun of it, you see. But he was a very good actor, that's the point.

DI NOLLI As a madman he's even more impressive, magnificent, terrifying.

BELCREDI From the word go. Imagine it, when the accident happened and he was thrown . . .

MATILDA It was dreadful. I was right next to him. I saw him under the hoofs, the horse bolting . . .

BELCREDI At first we didn't think he was seriously hurt. There was some commotion, and the cavalcade came to a halt. People wanted to know what had happened, but he'd already been picked up and carried into the house.

MATILDA There was nothing, not a scratch, no blood . . .

BELCREDI We thought he'd just passed out.

MATILDA Then, when a couple of hours later—

BELCREDI Yes—he showed up in the hall, that's what I was coming to.

MATILDA The look on his face—I noticed straight away.

BELCREDI No you didn't, none of us did. We didn't realise, you see . . .

MATILDA Well, of course *you* didn't—you were all acting like lunatics.

BELCREDI We were acting our parts, having fun; it was a beargarden.

MATILDA You can imagine the shock when we realised he wasn't pretending.

DOCTOR Ah, you mean, because he . . .

BELCREDI   Yes, he joined in. We thought he'd recovered and was acting up like the rest of us—and better than us, because, as I said, he was very good. We thought he was playing along with everyone else.

MATILDA   They started flicking him with their whips . . .

BELCREDI   And then he drew his sword. He was armed as a king, of course. He started slashing his sword around at people . . . a terrifying moment for all of us.

MATILDA   I'll never forget it, those faces . . . distorted, appalled in the face of his fury, which was no longer a masquerade but madness unmasked—

BELCREDI   Henry IV himself, in a towering rage.

MATILDA   He'd been obsessed with the pageant for a month or more—it occupied him in everything he did. I'm sure that was part of the reason.

BELCREDI   And the way he did his homework! Every detail, no matter how trivial.

DOCTOR   Well, it's classic. Fall from horse—hits head—brain damage—temporary obsession made permanent, fixed, causing a disturbance of the balance of the mind . . . up to insanity itself.

BELCREDI   (*to Frida and Di Nolli*)   See what life has got up its sleeve, my darlings? (*to Di Nolli*) You must have been four or five. (*to Frida*) Your mother had her portrait done before she had any idea that one day she'd have a daughter who'd replace her in it. And I've gone grey. As for him, (*pointing at the portrait*) one bang on the head and time stops, he's Henry IV.

DOCTOR   So, ladies and gentlemen, to sum up—

But Bertold enters looking upset.

BERTOLD   Sorry! . . .

FRIDA (*panicked*)   It's him!

MATILDA   Is it him?

BERTOLD   Sorry.

DI NOLLI   No—it's all right . . .

DOCTOR   Who is he?

BELCREDI   A leftover from our masquerade.

DI NOLLI   He's one of the young men we have here to keep him company.

BERTOLD   I'm sorry, Your Lordship—

DI NOLLI   Sorry! I gave orders we were not to be disturbed!

BERTOLD   Yes, sir, but I can't take any more, I want to give notice.

DI NOLLI   Oh, you're the one who was joining today.

BERTOLD   Yes, sir, and what I'm telling you is, I've had enough.

MATILDA   So he's not as calm as you made out.

BERTOLD   No, my lady, it's not him, it's those other three—talk about him needing humouring, Your Lordship, they're the crazy ones round here—

Landolf and Harold enter in a hurry, anxious, but stop at the threshold.

LANDOLF   Can we come in?

HAROLD   Begging your pardon, sir . . .

DI NOLLI   Come in!—What's going on? What do you think you're doing?

FRIDA (*scared*)   I'm going, I don't like this—

DI NOLLI   Don't, Frida . . .

LANDOLF   My lord, this fool . . .

BERTOLD   Oh, thanks very much—

HAROLD   He ruined everything, sir, by barging out of there—

LANDOLF   Himself is now beside himself, we can't hold him, he's ordered his arrest and wants to pronounce sentence from the throne—what should we do?

DI NOLLI   Lock the door!

Harold goes and locks the door.

HAROLD   Ordulf can't hold him on his own.

LANDOLF   My lord, maybe if we announce them right away, to distract him . . . Do you gentlemen know who you are going to be?

DI NOLLI   Yes, it's all decided . . . (*to the Doctor*) If you're ready, Doctor . . .

FRIDA   Well, I'm not, Carlo! I'm going—please come, Mother, please . . .

DOCTOR   I say, he's not armed, is he?

DI NOLLI   Of course not! Frida, don't be a baby—you wanted to come.

FRIDA   No I didn't, it was Mummy.

MATILDA Well, I'm ready. What do we have to do?

BELCREDI Is it really necessary for me to dress up?

LANDOLF Absolutely essential, sir! Look at us. I'm afraid there'll be hell to pay if he saw you dressed like that.

HAROLD He'd think it's the work of the devil.

LANDOLF What's worse he might think it's the work of his deadly enemy.

BELCREDI Gregory VII!

LANDOLF Exactly. He calls him the anti-Christ.

BELCREDI The Pope?—that's a good one.

LANDOLF Yes sir—and says he brings the dead to life, practises all the diabolical arts—he's terrified of him.

DOCTOR Paranoia, quite normal.

HAROLD He'd lose control.

DI NOLLI (*to Belcredi*) We can wait outside—it's only the Doctor who has to see him.

DOCTOR What, you mean on my own?

DI NOLLI They'll be with you!

DOCTOR Ah, no, I thought the Countess . . .

MATILDA I do—I am—I'm staying—of course I'm staying, I want to see him again!

FRIDA What for, Mummy?—please come . . .

MATILDA (*imperiously*) Stop it—this is what I came for. (*to Landolf*) I'll be . . . the mother-in-law, Adelaide.

LANDOLF   Right. Bertha's mother, fine, you won't need any more than a cloak and a coronet . . . (*to Harold*) Get on with it, Harry.

HAROLD   What about the Doctor?

DOCTOR   Yes . . . we thought, the Bishop . . . Bishop Hugo of Cluny.

HAROLD   Abbot of Cluny, sir—right . . .

LANDOLF   He's been here lots of times.

DOCTOR   Lots of . . . ?

LANDOLF   No problem, it's a simple costume.

DOCTOR   But . . .

LANDOLF   He won't remember you, he doesn't take in faces, only the clothes.

MATILDA   That should help.

DI NOLLI   We'll go, Frida—come on, Tito.

BELCREDI   If she's staying, I'm staying.

MATILDA   I don't need you here.

BELCREDI   I didn't say you needed me—I'd like to see him again, too, any objections?

LANDOLF   It might look better if there were three of you.

HAROLD   So, what's he . . . ?

BELCREDI   Oh, just find something simple for me . . .

LANDOLF (*to Harold*)   A Clunatic.

BELCREDI   A Clunatic? What's that?

LANDOLF The Abbot of Cluny's retinue—in a Benedictine habit. (*to Harold*) Go, go! (*to Bertold*) You, too, Bertold— and keep out of sight for the rest of the day. No—wait—(*to Bertold*) bring in the costumes he gives you. (*to Harold*) And then go and announce they're coming—Duchess Adelaide and Monsignor Hugo of Cluny, got it?

HAROLD Got it!

Harold and Bertold exit.

DI NOLLI We'll make ourselves scarce.

Di Nolli and Frida exit.

DOCTOR (*to Landolf*) He likes me, doesn't he?—I mean, Hugo of Cluny?

LANDOLF Yes, don't worry, Monsignor has always been received with the greatest respect here. You don't worry yourself either, my lady. He never forgets that you both spoke up for him when he'd been waiting two days in the snow, half frozen outside Canossa and the Pope let him in finally . . .

BELCREDI And what about me?

LANDOLF You just keep back and act respectful.

MATILDA I wish you'd wait outside.

BELCREDI Aren't you getting a bit . . . ?

MATILDA Whatever I'm getting, I'm getting. Leave me alone.

Bertold returns with the garments.

LANDOLF Ah—wardrobe! The cloak for the Countess.

MATILDA Wait, I'll take off my hat.

LANDOLF (*to Bertold*)   Lose the hat. (*to Matilda*) May I?

MATILDA   Aren't there any mirrors here?

LANDOLF   Outside. If Your Ladyship would rather see to herself . . . ?

MATILDA   That would be better. Let me have it; I'll be back in a minute.

Matilda takes her hat and goes out with Bertold, who is carrying her cloak and coronet. Meanwhile the Doctor and Belcredi put on the Benedictine robes as best they can.

BELCREDI   I wasn't frankly expecting to join the Benedictines. It's a pretty expensive form of insanity, this!

DOCTOR   None of them come cheap.

BELCREDI   Yes, but when there's a fortune at one's disposal . . .

LANDOLF   You're right, sir—we have an entire costume department, everything perfectly made from period patterns. It's my personal responsibility to commission trained costumiers. We spend a mint.

Matilda reenters wearing cloak and coronet.

BELCREDI   Ah!—beautiful! You look like a queen.

MATILDA   You look like an ostrich in holy orders. Take it off.

BELCREDI   Have you seen the Doctor?

DOCTOR   I know, it's too bad . . . never mind . . .

MATILDA   No, the Doctor's fine . . . but you, you are ridiculous!

DOCTOR (*to Landolf*)   Does he receive people often?

LANDOLF   It depends. Sometimes he demands to see this or that character, and then we have to find somebody who's willing . . . Women, too.

MATILDA   Oh?—women, too?

BELCREDI   You don't say. In costume? (*pointing at Matilda*) Like that?

LANDOLF   Well, you know, women who'll do it.

BELCREDI   Ah. (*to Matilda*) Watch yourself—this could be tricky.

Harold enters, gesturing for silence.

HAROLD   His Majesty the Emperor!

Ordulf and Harold take their positions. Ordulf holds the imperial crown, Harold the sceptre with the eagle and the orb with the cross. HENRY IV enters.

HENRY (*bowing*)   My lady . . . Monsignor . . .

Henry sees Belcredi, and is about to bow to him too, but turns to Landolf, and whispers.

HENRY (*cont.*)   Isn't that Peter Damian?

LANDOLF   No, Your Majesty, he's a monk from Cluny attending the Abbot.

HENRY   Peter Damian! It's no good looking to the Duchess, Peter!
      On my oath, Duchess, I've had a change of heart toward your daughter. I admit I wanted to divorce her and would have done if he hadn't stopped me—because there were others who'd have played along—the Bishop of Mainz, for one, he was willing for a hundred and twenty farms . . . (*He*

glances at Landolf, a little lost, and quickly says:) Still, I
shouldn't be speaking ill of clerics here . . . (*becoming humble
again with Belcredi*) I'm grateful now, believe me, I'm
grateful to you for stopping me. My life has been one
humiliation after another . . . and now here I am in
sackcloth, as you see. (*suddenly changing tone*) Bear up. No
matter—clear head, keen eye, straight back—come what
may—(*resuming*) I know how to correct my path where I
have erred—I'll even prostrate myself before you, Peter
Damian. I take it it's not you who's been putting it about
that my saintly mother spread her legs for the Bishop of
Augsburg?

BELCREDI   Er, no, that wasn't me.

HENRY   Ha! The nerve of it. (*staring at Belcredi*) No, I don't
think you've got it in you. (*tugging the Doctor's sleeve*) It's
always "them," isn't that so, Monsignor?

HAROLD (*quietly prompting the Doctor*)   Oh yes, those grasping
bishops . . .

DOCTOR   Right, yes . . . them . . .

HENRY   They'd stop at nothing. Poor little boy that I was,
playing with my toys, a king and didn't know it . . . I was
six when they tore me away from my mother, an innocent
to be used against her, against the dynasty itself . . .
profaning, picking and stealing . . .

LANDOLF   Your Majesty . . .

HENRY   Yes, all right. But these disgraceful slanders against
my mother is going too far.
      I cannot even mourn her, Duchess. I turn to you because
you must have a mother's heart. She came to see me, from
her convent, a month ago. They tell me she's dead. (*smiling*

sadly) But I can't grieve for her, because if you're here and I'm in sackcloth, that means I'm twenty-six.

HAROLD (*whispering, comforting*)   So it follows she can't be dead, Your Majesty.

HENRY   So I'll grieve for her all in good time.

Henry shows Matilda his hair colour, almost coquettishly.

HENRY (*cont.*)   Look!—still blond! (*confidentially*) For you. I don't care for myself. Though it helps . . . a little touch . . . trim the sails of time, you follow me, Monsignor?

Henry goes to look at her hair.

HENRY (*cont.*)   Oh, I see that you, too . . . Italians! *Tsk!* Far be it for me to criticize . . . None of us likes to acknowledge the mortality that sets limits to our will. But if you're born you die, that's what I say! Did you ask to be born, Monsignor? I didn't. And between birth and death, neither of our choosing, many things happen we wouldn't have chosen, which reluctantly—we have to live with.

DOCTOR (*studying Henry closely*)   True . . . sad but true . . .

HENRY   You see, when we refuse to resign ourselves, what's the result? Wishful thinking at its most futile. A woman who wishes she were a man . . . an old man who wishes he were young . . . None of us lies or pretends—what happens is, in all sincerity, we inhabit the self we have chosen for ourselves, and don't let go. But while you're holding tight, gripping on to your monk's robe, Monsignor, from out your sleeve something slips away without you noticing: your life! And how surprised you'll be when you suddenly see it going, gone—how you'll despise yourself—and how sorry you'll be, oh yes, if you only knew how often I've grieved over mine, slithering off—it had my face but was so disfigured I had to turn away.

Henry approaches Matilda.

HENRY (*cont.*)   Has that never happened to you, my lady? Do you think of yourself unchanging and unchanged? Oh God, but there was a day . . . How could you? How could you have done that?

He stares into Matilda's eyes.

HENRY (*cont.*)   Yes—that. We understand each other. Don't worry, it's our secret. And you, Peter Damian . . . that you could be friends with someone like that!

LANDOLF   Your Majesty . . .

HENRY   No names. I know how upset people get.

Henry turns to Belcredi.

HENRY (*cont.*)   Do you agree? We all hug our idea of ourselves to ourselves. As our hair turns greyer, we keep pace with the colouring bottle. It's of no consequence that I fool nobody. You, Duchess, don't fool yourself or anybody else—perhaps the image in your mirror, just a tiny bit. I do it to amuse myself. You do it in earnest. But no amount of earnestness stops it being a masquerade, and I'm not referring to your cloak and coronet. I'm talking about a memory of yourself you want to hold tight, the memory of a day gone by when to be fair-haired was your delight—or dark-haired if you were dark: the faded memory of being young. With you, it's different, Peter Damian. The memory of who you were, what you did, is no more than a dream that's safe with you—isn't that so?—a bad dream. It's the same for me. Dreams, many of them, now I think of it, with no meaning I can explain. Oh, well!—nothing to be done, and tomorrow will be more of the same.

Henry flies into a sudden fury, grabbing the sackcloth he's wearing.

HENRY (*cont.*)   This sackcloth . . . !

Then with a wild joy, Henry makes as if to rip the sackcloth off, while Harold and Ordulf, frightened, rush to stop him.

HENRY (*cont.*)   Oh God!
  (*backing away, shouting, taking off his sackcloth*) Tomorrow in Brixen, twenty-seven bishops from Germany and Lombardy will sign my petition for the removal of that impostor Gregory VII!

ORDULF   Your Majesty, please, for God's sake . . .

HAROLD (*urging him with signs to put his sackcloth back on*)   Don't say that Your Majesty . . . The Abbot's here with the Duchess to intercede on your behalf.

Surreptitiously Harold makes signs to the Doctor, urging him to say something quickly.

DOCTOR (*confused*)   Ah—yes—that's it—we're here to intercede . . .

Henry allows the three Counsellors to put the sackcloth back on his shoulders.

HENRY   Yes—forgive me . . . God be my witness, it's the burden of excommunication lying on me like a dead weight . . . Forgive me . . . my lady . . . Monsignor . . . (*quietly to Landolf, Harold, and Ordulf*) I don't know what it is, but I just can't bring myself to grovel to that man.

LANDOLF   That's because, Your Majesty, you've convinced yourself he's Peter Damian when he isn't!

HENRY He isn't?

HAROLD No, he's just some poor monk, Your Majesty.

HENRY We're none of us the best judge of our actions when we act on instinct. Perhaps it takes a woman to understand me. Think of your daughter, Duchess—think of Bertha—I told you how my heart has changed.

Henry suddenly turns to Belcredi and shouts in his face, as if he had denied it.

HENRY (*cont.*) Changed—changed—by the love and devotion she has shown me at this terrible time!

Henry stops, shaken by his own outburst of fury, and tries to contain himself, with a cry of exasperation in his throat; then he turns back to Matilda, in gentle and sorrowful humility.

HENRY (*cont.*) She's come with me, my lady, she's waiting in the courtyard. She chose to follow me like a beggar, and she's frozen from two nights out in the snow! You're her mother, doesn't it stir you to pity?—to go with him (*He points at the Doctor.*) and implore the Pope to receive me and grant forgiveness?

MATILDA (*shaking*) Oh, yes . . . yes . . . and at once . . .

DOCTOR We'll do it! We'll do it!

HENRY And another thing! One more thing!

Henry calls them all round him and whispers in great secret.

HENRY (*cont.*) Receiving me is not enough. The Pope can do . . . anything. Even raise the dead. (*beating his chest*) Well, here I am. As you see me. There's no magic he can't overcome. My real punishment is this—

Henry points at his picture on the wall, almost fearful.

30

HENRY (*cont.*) That!—look at it—to be shackled to that apparition! I'm a penitent now and a penitent I'll remain, I swear to God, until His Holiness receives me. But once the anathema has been lifted, please, both of you, beg the Pope to do this one thing, because he can do it: set me free from that, there, so that—wretched as it is—I can live my own life. (*pointing at the picture on the wall*) You can't stay twenty-six forever! I'm asking this for your daughter, too—so I can love her as she deserves to be loved.

There. That's it. I am in your hands.

(*bowing*) My lady! Monsignor!

Henry heads back still bowing, but then he notices Belcredi, who has come closer to listen: he fears he may want to steal the imperial crown, which is sitting on the throne. Henry rushes to pick it up and hide it under his sackcloth. Then, with a sly smile he bows repeatedly and exits. Matilda is so shocked she collapses into a chair, almost fainting.

ACT TWO

*Another room in the villa, adjoining the throne room, furnished in a
plain antique style. Late afternoon of the same day. Onstage are
Matilda, the Doctor, and Belcredi. Matilda is keeping apart,
preoccupied and on edge.*

BELCREDI   Well . . . pretty straightforward so far, wouldn't
you say? a) He's off his trolley and b) he smelled a rat. He
wasn't fooled . . . He told us himself in so many words. (*to
Matilda*) You heard him, didn't you?

MATILDA   What . . . ? Yes, but it wasn't what you think.

DOCTOR   He responded to our costumes the way a child
would.

MATILDA   A child? What are you talking about?

DOCTOR   On one level. On another it's more complicated
than you can imagine.

MATILDA   Not to me—it was plain as day.

DOCTOR   To you, perhaps, but we must bear in mind the
peculiar psychology of the mad—they can see right through
any pretence, while at the same time suspending their
disbelief, like children at play believing in their make-
believe. That's why I say he is in one sense like a child
while in another it's complicated—because, you see, *his*
make-believe—and he is well aware of it—is that he is the
image of that image in the picture frame.

BELCREDI   He did say that.

DOCTOR   There you are. Then what happens?—his image is
joined by other images: us, do you follow me? And with

32

that shrewd insight of the madman, he immediately spotted the difference between us and him; he spotted the pretence, which made him suspicious. But he kept his suspicions to himself. That's what madmen do. And that's all there is to it! Of course, he didn't see that we were doing it all for his sake. What made the game all the more pitiful is that he kept trying, in his coy, obstinate way, to tell us it was only a game—*his* game—hence the makeup and how he only puts it on for fun, and so on.

MATILDA   No, you haven't got it.

DOCTOR   What do you . . . ?

MATILDA   The plain fact is he recognised me.

DOCTOR   That's impossible.

BELCREDI (*at the same time*)   He couldn't have.

MATILDA   I'm telling you he recognised me. When he looked into my eyes, he knew me.

BELCREDI   But he was talking to you about Bertha, your daughter.

MATILDA   He was talking about me—me!

BELCREDI   Well, yes, he did mention . . .

MATILDA   My dyed hair, exactly—and how quickly he added—didn't you notice?—"or dark-haired if you were dark." He remembered perfectly well that back then my hair was dark.

BELCREDI   No, no . . .

MATILDA (*to the Doctor*)   My hair is naturally dark, like Frida's. That's what got him talking about my daughter.

33

BELCREDI   What daughter? He's never seen your daughter.

MATILDA   That's my point, you idiot—everything he said about my pretend daughter *now,* he was saying about me *then!*

BELCREDI   It's catching!

MATILDA   Oh, don't be so stupid.

BELCREDI   Excuse me but when were you ever his wife? He's got a wife—in his mad mind she's Bertha of Susa and you're her mother.

MATILDA   I'm not denying that I came to him as Adelaide— being blond and not dark anymore, the way he remembered me, I decided to be the mother-in-law. But the daughter doesn't exist for him. He's never seen her. He doesn't even know I've got a daughter—so how can he know what colour her hair is?

BELCREDI   He didn't say he knew. He was just speaking generally . . . Good God, he was only making a point about people colouring their hair to look younger than they are— blondes, brunettes . . . and as usual you go off at a tangent.

MATILDA   No . . . no . . . I don't care what you say, he was talking to me about me, everything he said . . .

BELCREDI   I couldn't get a word in edgeways, and it was all about you!—what?—even when he was talking to Peter Damian?

MATILDA   Indirectly, yes. Or perhaps you have another explanation why he took an instant dislike to you?

DOCTOR   (*after an awkward pause*)   Well, perhaps it was simply that it was only Duchess Adelaide and the Abbot of Cluny who were announced . . . and seeing there was a third person there made him mistrustful.

BELCREDI   There you are. His mistrust made him leery of me, and she has to insist it was because he recognised her.

MATILDA   Well, he did! You know that look where you just *know*. It was just a flash . . . I don't know how to put it . . .

DOCTOR   A moment of lucidity . . .

MATILDA   Yes! And from then on everything he said seemed to be steeped in regret, for his youth, and mine, because of the awful thing that happened to him, that froze him in that mask he longs to be free of.

BELCREDI   Oh, yes!—free to love your daughter, as he said— or, in your version, to love you—touched by your compassion perhaps?

MATILDA   And compassion is very much what I'm feeling, believe me.

BELCREDI   Oh, I do!—it's like a miracle.

DOCTOR   May I speak? We doctors don't deal in miracles. I listened very carefully to everything he said, and, as I would put it, there's a relaxation in the coherence typical of systematised delusion; it's clearly, how can I put it, relaxed; the coherence of the delusion isn't er, cohering as before. He can't quite find the point of equilibrium between ego and superego . . . A sudden memory deflects him, not—and this is very encouraging—not into incipient inertia but rather into a melancholic reflex, which indicates . . . yes, significant cerebral activity. As I say, very encouraging. Now, with the shock tactic we have decided on—

MATILDA   Why isn't the car back? It's over three hours . . .

DOCTOR   What?

MATILDA   The car! It's been over three hours!

DOCTOR (*looking at his watch*)   Four, actually.

MATILDA   It should have been back ages ago. But as usual . . .

DOCTOR   Maybe they can't find the dress.

MATILDA   I told them exactly where it was. And where's Frida?

BELCREDI   In the garden with Carlo.

DOCTOR   Calming her nerves.

BELCREDI   It wasn't nerves, it was a tantrum.

MATILDA   Don't try to force her, believe me, I know her.

DOCTOR   Let's not rush things. We have to wait till it's dark, and it won't take a minute to set up. If we can give him a shock and snap the thread which binds him to his delusion, give him back what he longs for—he said it himself; you can't stay twenty-six for ever!—and free him from his prison—that's the way he sees it—

BELCREDI   —he'll be cured! Saved by the alienation technique!

DOCTOR   His clock stopped, and we're checking our watches for the critical moment when . . . with a quick shake, we might get his clock ticking again, after all this time.

Di Nolli enters.

MATILDA   Carlo! Where's Frida?

DI NOLLI   She's coming.

DOCTOR   Is the car back?

DI NOLLI   Yes.

MATILDA   It is? With the dress?

DI NOLLI   It's been back a while.

DOCTOR   Excellent!

MATILDA   Well, where is she? And the dress . . . ?

DI NOLLI   You'll see in a moment. Here she comes.

BERTOLD (*entering*)   Her Highness the Countess of Canossa!

Frida enters, the image of the portrait.

FRIDA   Of Tuscany, if you don't mind. Canossa is just one of my castles.

BELCREDI   Just look at her! Look at her! She's a different person.

MATILDA   She's me! My God, can you see? Stop there, Frida! She's my portrait come to life!

DOCTOR   Yes . . . Perfect!

BELCREDI   It's amazing.

FRIDA   Don't anybody make me laugh or I'll burst. Was your waist really so tiny, Mummy? I'm having to hold my stomach in.

MATILDA   Wait . . . Hold still . . . These creases, is it really that tight on you?

FRIDA   I can barely breathe. You better make it quick . . .

DOCTOR   But we have to wait till dark . . .

FRIDA   I can't hold myself in till dark!

MATILDA   Why did you put it on so early?

37

FRIDA I couldn't resist. The minute I saw it . . .

DOCTOR Would you stand over there . . . here . . . not quite so close . . . now forward just a little . . .

BELCREDI For the full effect of twenty years between.

MATILDA What a disaster, eh?

BELCREDI Oh, I wouldn't go as far as that.

DOCTOR No, not at all! I only meant the dress . . . I meant . . . to compare . . .

BELCREDI As for the dress, it's not twenty years; more like a thousand. That's some shake for anybody's clock. (*pointing first at Frida and then at the Countess*) From there to there? You'll have to pick him up with a spoon. Think about it. Seriously: for us it's twenty years, two dresses, a masquerade . . . but if time stopped for him nearly a thousand years ago . . . Oh, you don't think so?

DOCTOR No. Because life doesn't stop. When the illusion is stripped away, you've caught up—the jump is not a thousand years, it's only twenty.

BELCREDI I've had a thought. Look at Frida and her mother. Who's leading the way? The older generation, that's who. The young think they're in the lead but they've got it backwards. We're years ahead of them, because we've been at it longer.

DOCTOR Ah, if only time didn't come between us like a wedge!

BELCREDI It doesn't. Young people still have to go through what we went through . . . get older, make more or less the same mistakes. It's an illusion that death is a doorway somewhere ahead of the door you came in by. You're

38

dying the moment you're born . . . those who started first are beating the path for those who follow. Look at her! (*He points at Frida.*)—centuries ahead of us, the Countess Matilda of Tuscany.

DI NOLLI Please. Tito—stop fooling.

BELCREDI Oh, you think I'm fooling?

DI NOLLI Ever since you got here.

BELCREDI Me? I even dressed up as a monk for you. I promise you, Doctor, I still don't understand what you're up to.

DOCTOR You will. Mind you, not with the Countess still dressed like that . . .

BELCREDI Ah—you mean, she, too . . . will have to . . .

DOCTOR Of course! Wearing a similar dress, which we've got ready for her, so he thinks she's the Countess Matilda of Canossa, too.

FRIDA Tuscany, Tuscany!

BELCREDI Oh . . . I see. He'll be confronted by two . . .

DOCTOR Exactly. Two of them. And then . . .

FRIDA (*with Di Nolli*) Two of who?

DI NOLLI I think he means . . .

DOCTOR (*joining them*) It's quite simple . . .

The three of them confer silently.

BELCREDI (*to Matilda*) My God . . . So then . . .

MATILDA Then what?

39

BELCREDI   Does he mean so much to you? To lend yourself to this farrago? It's quite something for a woman to . . .

MATILDA   For most women, perhaps.

BELCREDI   Oh no, my dear, for any woman! To demean herself . . .

MATILDA   I feel responsible.

BELCREDI   No you don't. You know you'd never suffer the indignity.

MATILDA   So if I wouldn't, what are you talking about? Where's the indignity?

BELCREDI   Oh, not so as *they'd* ever notice, just enough to humiliate me.

MATILDA   As if anyone's thinking of you at this moment!

DI NOLLI   Right—we're all set . . . (*to Bertold*) You—get one of those three in here.

BERTOLD (*leaving*)   Right away.

MATILDA   But first we have to pretend our characters are leaving.

DI NOLLI   Quite so—that's why I've called him to announce your departure. (*to Belcredi*) There's no need for you to be there.

BELCREDI   Naturally . . . no need for me . . . no need at all . . .

DI NOLLI   And anyway you might arouse his suspicion again, you see?

BELCREDI   I do see. A bit part.

Landolf, followed by Bertold, enters from the door on the right.

LANDOLF   Excuse me . . .

DI NOLLI   Come in, come in . . . You're Lolo, aren't you?

LANDOLF   Lolo or Landolpho, my lord, I answer to both.

DI NOLLI   Good. Now, the Doctor and the Countess will take their leave . . .

LANDOLF   No problem. We'll tell him the Pope's agreed to receive them. Himself's in his quarters sorry for everything he said and worrying His Holiness won't give him absolution. If you'd be so good, now put the costumes back on . . .

DOCTOR   Yes—right—let's get on with it.

LANDOLF   One other thing, if I may suggest. Tell him the Countess Matilda of Tuscany is all for it, begging the Pope on Himself's behalf.

MATILDA   You see? He did recognise me!

LANDOLF   No. Excuse me. It's only that what with His Holiness being under the Countess's roof, Himself is frightened it'll wreck his chances. It's a funny thing—you'll know better than me—but so far as I can see there's nothing in the history books about Henry IV being secretly in love with Matilda of Tuscany.

MATILDA   No, there isn't. On the contrary.

LANDOLF   That's what I thought. But he's always saying how he loved her, and now he's terrified her hating him might do for him with the Pope.

BELCREDI   Well, we must find a way to convince him that this aversion of hers is a thing of the past!

LANDOLF Fine. I'll tell him that.

MATILDA Yes, why don't you? (*to Belcredi*) Because, in case you didn't know, my dear, history records precisely that— the Pope yielded to the entreaties of Matilda and the Abbot of Cluny . . . and if you want to know, at the time, during the pageant, my intention was to remind him . . . to show him my feelings were not as unfriendly as he imagined.

BELCREDI Well, how wonderful . . . to have history on your side.

LANDOLF Well, if that's the case, why dress up twice over—? you could go in with the Monsignor dressed as the Countess of Tuscany.

DOCTOR No!—for God's sake! That would ruin everything! He's got to see the two of them together. Come along, there's no time to lose. Listen, my lady, you're still the mother-in-law, Adelaide. We leave. He sees us go. That's vital.

Landolf, Matilda, and the Doctor leave.

FRIDA I'm starting to feel nervous.

DI NOLLI Not again?

FRIDA It wouldn't be so bad if I'd seen him earlier.

DI NOLLI There's nothing to be afraid of.

FRIDA He's not going to be violent?

DI NOLLI No—he's perfectly calm.

BELCREDI Melancholic. Haven't you heard he's secretly in love with you?

FRIDA That's what worries me.

BELCREDI He won't hurt you.

DI NOLLI It'll be over before you know it.

FRIDA Yes, but alone with him, and it'll be dark . . .

DI NOLLI I'll be close by—and the others will be behind the door waiting, ready to rush in. As soon as he sees your mother, your part's over.

BELCREDI What *I'm* afraid of, on the other hand, is that it'll all be for nothing.

DI NOLLI Oh, don't you start! I have every faith in this cure.

FRIDA So have I. I'm getting quite excited.

BELCREDI But, you see, darlings, what we're forgetting is that madmen, though sadly they don't know it, bless them . . . don't think rationally!

DI NOLLI What's that got to do with anything?

BELCREDI What!—when he sees her (*pointing at Frida*) and then her mother, aren't we counting on him to apply his reason?—we've orchestrated the whole thing just for that.

DI NOLLI What do you mean, reason? The Doctor's just confronting him with his own make-believe doubled up, that's all.

BELCREDI For the life of me I can never understand why these people are allowed to call themselves doctors.

DI NOLLI What people?

BELCREDI Psychiatrists. Why do they graduate in *medicine*?

DI NOLLI What else should they graduate in?

43

BELCREDI Linguistics . . . It's only about who has the best lines . . . "coherence typical of systematised delusion" . . . "melancholic reflex" . . . The first thing they tell you is they don't perform miracles when a miracle is exactly what's needed—they know that's how to be taken seriously . . . and the miracle is they get away with it.

BERTOLD (*peeping*) They're coming! Coming this way!

DI NOLLI Are you sure?

BERTOLD It looks like he's seeing them out! Yes . . . here he comes!

DI NOLLI Let's get out of here. You stay.

BERTOLD Me?

Di Nolli, Frida, and Belcredi hurry out, leaving Bertold behind, confused and lost. Landolf enters bowing, followed by Matilda, with cloak and coronet, as in Act One, and the Doctor, in the robes of the Abbot of Cluny. Henry IV is between them, in regal attire, followed by Ordulf and Harold.

HENRY I'm asking you: do you think I'm mulish or foxy? (*pause*) A mule, then.

DOCTOR A mule? Heaven forbid that I . . .

HENRY So you think I'm really a fox?

DOCTOR No, not a mule and not a fox either.

HENRY Come, Abbot, since one can't be both I was hoping that in denying me the obstinacy of the one you'd grant me the cleverness of the other. I assure you I could do with a little of it. But I suppose you reserve it all for yourself.

DOCTOR Who, me? Do I seem clever to you?

44

HENRY No, Monsignor! What an idea! (*addressing Matilda*) Could you spare me a moment before you go? (*anxiously, in private*) Do you truly love your daughter?

MATILDA Yes, of course I do . . .

HENRY So, do you wish me to love and cherish her to make up for all the wrongs I've done her? . . . not that you should credit the debauchery my enemies accuse me of.

MATILDA I don't. I never did.

HENRY Well, then, what would you have me do?

MATILDA What?

HENRY Fall in love with your daughter again? (*pauses, looks at her intently*) Watch out for the Countess of Tuscany—she's not to be trusted.

MATILDA But—as I told you—she's begged and beseeched His Holiness no less than we have . . .

HENRY Don't say that! Don't! Can't you see what it does to me?

Matilda looks at him and speaks to him quietly, sharing a confidence.

MATILDA Do you still love her?

HENRY Still? What do you mean, still? Nobody knows about that—nobody must know it.

MATILDA But perhaps she knows . . . and that's why she went on her knees to the Pope for you . . .

HENRY And you say you love your daughter! (*pause; lightly*) Well, Monsignor! It's all too true, about me finding out too late—far too late . . . that I had a wife . . . and still have her, there's no doubt about that . . . and I swear I never give her a thought. It may be a sin but I feel nothing for her. What's astonishing, though, is neither does her mother! Admit it, Duchess, you don't give a damn about her. (*agitated*) She keeps on about that other woman! She goes on and on about her—I can't think why.

LANDOLF Perhaps, Your Majesty, it's because she thinks you've got the wrong idea about the Countess of Tuscany. (*embarrassed*) I mean the wrong idea just at the present time.

HENRY Why, do you think I can trust her, too?

LANDOLF At the present time I do, Your Majesty.

MATILDA You see? And that's why . . .

HENRY Yes, I see. So, it's not that you think I love her. I see. I see. Nobody has ever thought so. So much the better. So that's enough about that.

Henry stops. He turns to the Doctor with a completely different mood and expression.

HENRY (*cont.*) Monsignor, did you notice this?—the conditions the Pope has made for the revoking of my excommunication have absolutely nothing to do with the reason he excommunicated me in the first place. Tell Pope Gregory we'll meet in Brixen. And you, my lady, if you happen to see your daughter in the castle courtyard of your friend the Countess . . . what can I say? Tell her she can come up here. We'll see whether she's the one who'll stay by me as wife and Empress. I've had lots of them coming here assuring me that they were her . . . though they knew I'd already . . . and sometimes I'd . . . well, why not?—it's my wife! But they all . . . when they'd tell me they were Bertha, and from Susa . . . I don't know why, they'd all start giggling. (*confidentially*) You know

46

what I mean—in bed—not dressed up like this—the woman, too, naked . . . stripped down to male and female as nature made us, we forget who we are. Our clothes hanging up, watching over us like ghosts . . . (*to the Doctor*) What I think, Monsignor, is that ghosts for the most part are fragments of the unconscious escaping from our dreams. When we sometimes see them wide-awake, in broad daylight, they startle us. I'm always frightened in the night when they appear—all those disjointed images, people laughing, riders got down from their horses . . . I'm frightened sometimes by the blood pounding through my veins in the stillness of the night, like the heavy thud of footsteps in distant rooms . . . But I've kept you in attendance long enough. My respects, Duchess, and Monsignor, your obedient servant.

Matilda and the Doctor bow in return, and leave. Henry closes the door and turns around, changed.

HENRY (*cont.*)   What a bunch of wankers! I played them like a kiddy piano with a different colour for every key—it only needed the lightest touch . . . white, red, yellow, green . . . and that other one, Peter Damian!—Ha! I saw through him all right! He didn't dare show his face again!

Henry, in an exuberant frenzy, suddenly sees Bertold, who is both stunned and frightened. Henry stops in front of him, pointing out Bertold to his three companions, and shakes him by the shoulders.

HENRY (*cont.*)   Look at this idiot here, with his mouth open! Do you understand now?—how I got them dressed up to perform for me?—those clowns wetting their pants in terror . . . in case I whip off their masks!—as if it wasn't me who made them dress up for my own entertainment while I play the madman!

47

LANDOLF, HAROLD, & ORDULF   Eh?—What?—What's he—?

HENRY   Well, I'm sick of this! Enough! You're all getting on
my tits! My God, the nerve of that woman!—showing up
here with her lover! With that air of stooping to this
charade out of the goodness of their hearts!—so as not to
make even madder a poor wretch already shut off from the
world, from life! Well, who else would put up with that
kind of persecution? These are people who every living
moment expect everyone else to be how they see them!—
oh, but this can't be persecution!—not at all!—it's only
their mode of thinking, living, feeling—each to his own!
And you to yours, right? Of course! But what is yours? To
be sheep!—feeble, flock-driven . . . and they make the most
of that, they have you seeing and thinking and feeling the
same as them. Or so they like to think. Because, when all's
said and done, what do they do it with? Words, words,
words. Simple words which anyone can make mean
whatever they like. That's what's called public opinion!
God help anyone who finds the public's got a word for him
. . . "crazy," or, I don't know, "imbecile"? Tell me
something. Would you be so calm if you knew that there
are people out there determined to make the world see you
the way they want you to be seen?—to force their view of
you and their valuation of you on everyone else? "Loony!"
"Crackpot!" Don't imagine I'm doing all this as a madman
now. Before I hit my head falling off a horse . . .

Henry suddenly stops, noticing the four young men are agitated,
dismayed, and confused.

HENRY (*cont.*)   Why are you staring at each other? Trying to
decide? Is he or isn't he? All right, then, I'm a loony!
Well, by God, on your knees, then! Kneel! I command

you to get on your knees and touch the ground with your foreheads, three times. Get down! That's what you do when you're confronted by a maniac! (*jeers*) Oh, get up for God's sake! Sheep! Why didn't you put me in a straitjacket? You're crushed by the weight of a word that weighs less than a fly. Our whole lives, crushed by the weight of words, empty words. Here I am. Hello. Do you really think Henry IV is alive? Yet, you're alive—and you let me order you about. Do you think it's funny, a dead man running your lives? Well, maybe it's funny in here. Go outside in the real world, and the joke wears a little thin. The day breaks—it's dawn, the day's ahead of us, you say, it's ours to make. Really? You really think so? Start talking. Repeat all the words that have ever been said. Do you think you're living now? Well, you're not. You're chewing on dead men's cud. (*stopping in front of Bertold, who is now completely dazed*) You haven't understood a thing, have you? What's your name?

BERTOLD   My name . . . er, Bertold.

HENRY   Bertold, my arse. Just between you and me, what's your name?

BERTOLD   Well, actually, it's Fino.

HENRY   Fino what?

BERTOLD   Fino Pagliuca, sir.

HENRY   I've often heard you using your names. You're Lolo?

LANDOLF   Yes, sir. (*joyfully*) Oh, my God, you mean . . . ?

HENRY (*sharply*)   I mean what?

LANDOLF   No . . . I only . . .

HENRY Aren't I crazy anymore? No, of course not, let's have a really good laugh at those who think I am. (*to Harold*) You're Franco . . . (*to Ordulf*) And you, let me think . . .

ORDULF Momo!

HENRY That's it! Momo! Nice name.

LANDOLF But then . . . Oh, God . . .

HENRY What? Nothing, let's have a good laugh about it, just the five of us. After three. Three. Ha, ha, ha, ha, ha!

Landolf, Harold, and Ordulf are unsure, confused, glad, and bewildered at the same time. They are whispering together.

HENRY (*cont.*) Stop that whispering! (*to Bertold*) You're not laughing? Did I offend you? I wasn't talking about you, you know. It's everyone. It suits them to make out that someone is crazy so they can shut him away. Do you know why? Because they can't bear to hear what he might say . . . what I might say about those three who just left. I might say one's a slut, one's a dirty lecher, and the third's a quack. Surely not!—who'd believe such a thing! Yet they'd all be listening, horrified. But why? If it's not true? That's what I'd like to know. You shouldn't believe a madman. But they listen, wide-eyed with horror. Explain that to me. Go on—I'm quite calm as you see.

BERTOLD Maybe . . . it's because they think . . .

HENRY No, no, look at me! I'm not saying it's true—nothing is true—but look into my eyes.

BERTOLD I am.

HENRY What do you see? Yourself. See? See the fear in your eyes? Because now you think I'm mad. I've proved my point.

LANDOLF What point?

HENRY You're staring because you think I'm crazy again.
Well, why wouldn't you, for heaven's sake? You've believed
it all this time, haven't you? Well, have you or haven't you?
(*He sees they are terrified.*) Feel it now?—the ground
disappearing under your feet, the air knocked out of your
body? What do you expect?—faced with a madman?—with
someone who shakes the foundations of everything you've
shored up, inside and out?—your logic! Right? Of course!
Madmen, lucky them, don't build logically. Or with the logic
of a feather on the breeze, this way, that way, day to day.
You hold everything tight; madmen let everything go. You
say: this can't be; madmen say: anything is possible! But now
you're thinking: not true. Because it's not true for you—and
you—and you—and to a hundred thousand others. All right,
take a look at what they think is the truth, the sane
majority—what a show they make with their common
ground, their wonderful logic. When I was a child, the moon
in the bottom of a well was real to me. And many other
things, too. I believed everything I was told and I was happy.
Heaven help you if you don't cling to your own reality, even
if yesterday's is contradicted by tomorrow's. Pray God you
don't find out the thing that'll drive anyone crazy: that when
you see yourself reflected in someone's eyes—as happened to
me once—you see a beggar standing at a gate he can never
enter. The one who goes in can never be you, in your
closed-off, self-created world . . . It's someone you don't
know, the one who is seen by the person who looks into *your*
eyes, and *his* world is closed off from yours. (*pause*) It's got
dark in here.

ORDULF (*eagerly*) Would you like me to fetch the lamp?

HENRY The lamp, yes . . . the lamp. Do you think I don't know that as soon as I turn my back, off to bed with my flickering lamp . . . you switch on the lights?—same thing in the throne room. I pretend not to notice.

ORDULF Ah, well, in that case, would you like . . .

HENRY No, it's blinding; I want my lamp.

ORDULF Fine—it's right outside.

Ordulf goes out, returning immediately with an antique lamp—one of those you hold by a ring on top.

HENRY Good. Shed a little light. Sit here. No, not bolt upright . . . make yourself comfortable . . . And I'll go here . . . Pity we can't order up a nice moonbeam. The moon is our friend. I often feel grateful to her . . . lost to myself, gazing up at her from my window . . . Who would believe that she knows nine hundred and twenty-seven years have gone by and I, sitting at my window like any poor fellow, can't really be Henry IV? I say, what a lovely picture we make: "The Emperor Among His Faithful Counsellors: Night." Isn't this nice?

LANDOLF (*quietly to Bertold*) Do you realise? If we'd only known it was all pretend . . .

HENRY What was?

LANDOLF Er . . . what I mean is . . . this morning I was just saying to him . . . (*He points at Bertold.*) because he's just joined . . . I was saying, what a shame, what with our costumes, and lots more in wardrobe, and with that great throne room . . .

HENRY What about it? What's a shame?

LANDOLF Well . . . that we never knew . . .

HENRY That this comedy was a comedy?

LANDOLF Because we thought . . .

HAROLD Yes, that it was all real.

HENRY And it isn't? You don't think it's real?

LANDOLF Well, if you're saying . . .

HENRY What I'm saying is that you're all stupid. You should have acted it for yourselves, not for my sake or the occasional visitor, but just like this, behaving naturally, with no one to see . . . eating, sleeping, scratching your arse, living, alive in the remote, romantic, sepulchral past, here at the court of Henry IV! And reflecting that nine hundred years on, there are people scuffling about in a permanent state of torment desperate to know how things will turn out for them. While you, meanwhile, are already history! Whatever happens has happened, however painful the events and brutal the battles, they're history and nothing can change them, they're fixed, forever . . . so you can sit back and admire how every cause leads obediently to its effect, with perfect logic, how every event fits neatly with every other. That's the wonderful thing about history.

LANDOLF Beautiful . . . beautiful . . .

HENRY Yes—but now it's over. Now that you're in on it I can't do it anymore. I can't take my flickering lamp to bed. I'm bored with it all! (*almost to himself, violent with contained anger*) By God, I'll make her sorry she came! Dressed up as my mother-in-law! And that Abbot! Dragging along a doctor to study me. Thought they'd cure me, did they? Idiots! I'd love to give at least one of them a hard slap—yes,

53

that one, a famous swordsman, I believe. He'll run me through! Well, we'll see, won't we . . . ?

There is a knock at the door.

HENRY (*cont.*) Who is it?

GIOVANNI (*offstage*) Deo gratis.

HAROLD Oh, it's Giovanni come to do his evening performance as the little monk!

ORDULF Good, let's make him do the whole thing!

HENRY (*sternly*) You foolish boy—you don't understand . . . making fun of a poor old man who's only doing this out of love for me.

LANDOLF (*to Ordulf*) We have to take it seriously.

HENRY Exactly. Deadly serious. Otherwise you're making a cheap joke of truth.

Henry opens the door and lets Giovanni in, dressed as a humble monk, with a parchment scroll under his arm.

HENRY (*cont.*) Come in, Father. (*continuing to them*) All the documents concerning my life and reign that had anything good to say about me were destroyed by my enemies. Nothing survived except this, my biography, written down by a humble and devoted monk . . . and you'd make fun of him? (*to Giovanni, fondly*) Sit down, Father . . . sit there and . . . keep the lamp by you.

Henry sets the oil lamp next to Giovanni.

HENRY (*cont.*) Ready?

GIOVANNI (*unrolling the parchment*) Ready, Your Majesty.

HENRY So, write . . . (*dictating*) "Henry IV's excommunication gave the barons their opportunity. On October sixteenth, 1076, at the diet of Tribur, they decreed that Henry would lose his kingdom if he did not receive absolution within a year and a day. But he escaped to Italy, and at Canossa in January 1077, in the castle of his enemy Matilda of Tuscany, he threw himself on the mercy of the Pope.

ACT THREE

The throne room is dark. The canvasses of the two paintings have been removed, and in their place, inside the frames, are Frida, dressed as "Countess of Tuscany," as we've seen her in Act Two and Carlo Di Nolli, dressed as "Henry IV," frozen in the same postures as the paintings. Henry IV enters, holding the lamp.

FRIDA Henry!

Henry stops at the sound of the voice and turns, frightened.

HENRY Who's that?

FRIDA *(slightly louder)* Henry!

Henry shrieks and drops the oil lamp, puts his arms around his head, and makes as if to run away. Frida jumps from the frame yelling like a madwoman.

FRIDA *(cont.)* Henry! Henry! I'm scared!

Di Nolli jumps down, rushing to Frida, who keeps on screaming, almost fainting.

DI NOLLI It's all right, Frida, it's me, I'm here . . .

From the door everybody rushes in: the Doctor, Matilda (dressed as "Countess of Tuscany"), Belcredi, Landolf, Harold, Ordulf, Bertold, and Giovanni. One of them switches on the lights in the room. Henry IV stands there watching, confused. The others, ignoring him, rush to help and comfort Frida, who is sobbing in the arms of her fiancé. They are all talking in great confusion.

BELCREDI *Finita la comedia!*

DOCTOR All over!

MATILDA He's made fools of us, Frida! Do you see?—he was cured all along!

DI NOLLI Cured?

BELCREDI It was all an act. Everything's all right.

FRIDA I'm so scared!

MATILDA There's nothing to be scared of now—look at him!

DI NOLLI What do you mean, cured?

DOCTOR So it seems, the two-faced . . .

BELCREDI That's right—(*pointing to the four Counsellors*) they told us all about it.

MATILDA He's been cured for ages—he confessed.

DI NOLLI But he's only just—this moment—

BELCREDI It was all put-on, he was laughing at you up his sleeve—us, too, for all our pains.

DI NOLLI I can't believe it!—making a fool of his own sister right up to her death?

Henry has remained, all hunched up, peeping out at them. He stands up and shouts at Di Nolli.

HENRY Go on! Yes? Keep going! Tell me more! Go on!

DI NOLLI (*startled*) Go on what?

HENRY She wasn't just "your sister" was she?

DI NOLLI My sister? I said *your* sister—you made her come here to the bitter end dressed up as your mother, Agnes!

HENRY Don't you mean *your* mother?

DI NOLLI *Of course* I mean my mother!

HENRY But your mother's been dead for centuries—you've just arrived fresh from there . . . jumping out newborn from your frame . . . How do you know I haven't been mourning her for years, in my heart, even dressed as I am?

MATILDA What's he talking about?

DOCTOR Calm down, everyone, please . . .

HENRY What am I talking about? I'm asking you, wasn't Agnes the mother of Henry IV? (*turning to Frida*) You should know, Countess, if anyone does.

FRIDA Me? I don't know anything!

DOCTOR He's having a relapse—stand back everyone.

BELCREDI Relapse, my eye! He's playing games again.

HENRY Me? Who was in the picture frames? Himself? Look at him, standing there—Henry IV.

BELCREDI We've had enough of this joke.

HENRY Who said it was a joke?

DOCTOR Don't provoke him, for God's sake.

BELCREDI They did! (*pointing again at the four Counsellors*) Them!

HENRY You? Did you tell them it was a joke?

LANDOLF No . . . we just said you were cured.

BELCREDI There you are. (*to Matilda*) Aren't you embarrassed at yourself?—look at him (*indicating Di Nolli*)—look at yourself, Countess—playing at dressing up!

MATILDA   Oh, shut up! What does it matter who's wearing what, if he's really cured?

HENRY   Yes, I'm really cured. (*to Belcredi*) But I haven't finished with you yet. (*aggressively*) Are you aware that in twenty years no one has dared to come into my presence dressed like you and this gentleman here?

Henry points to the Doctor.

BELCREDI   Of course I am. For that matter, when I appeared before you this morning I came dressed—

HENRY   —as a monk, of course!

BELCREDI   You mistook me for Peter Damian, and the only reason I didn't laugh was—

HENRY   You thought I was crazy. So, now that I'm sane, you can jeer at her to see her in costume? And yet, you might have reflected that, in my eyes, she looks . . . Oh, what does it matter? (*turning suddenly to the Doctor*) You're a doctor?

DOCTOR   Er—yes . . .

HENRY   So all this was your idea. Don't you realise you could have plunged my mind back onto the dark pit of madness . . . making pictures talk and leap out of their frames?

Henry observes Frida and Di Nolli, then Matilda, and lastly he looks at his own clothes.

HENRY (*cont.*)   Double, double . . . Splendid, just what the doctor ordered for the lunatic . . . (*pointing at Belcredi*) To him it's just another game of dressing up. (*addressing Belcredi*) And now—off with the motley, eh?—so I can come along with you—do you think?

BELCREDI   With me—with us . . .

HENRY Where should we go, then? How about the club? In best bib and tucker. Or shall we go home with the Countess, the two of us?

BELCREDI Whatever you like. Why not? You don't want to stay here—all alone and for evermore—keeping up a carnival joke that went wrong? It's amazing how you managed to keep it going once you'd recovered from the accident.

HENRY Ah, yes—but when the horse threw me and I hit my head, I actually did lose my mind, I'm not sure for how long.

DOCTOR Ah! Most interesting! How long roughly?

HENRY About twelve years. (*to Belcredi*) Yes—knowing nothing about what life had saved up for you and not for me, from the day of the carnival onwards . . . all the changes, friends who turned against me, or how my place was taken, in . . . let's say . . . the heart of a woman I loved . . . not knowing who'd died, who'd gone away . . . all that, you know, was no joke.

BELCREDI That's not what I said—I was talking about later when . . .

HENRY Oh—later! Well, one day . . . Are you listening, Doctor?—I'm a very interesting case, you should take notes . . . Well, one day . . . all by itself, God knows how, the damage here (*He touches his forehead.*) . . . mended itself . . . I open my eyes slowly, to begin with I'm not sure if I'm asleep or awake—and then, yes, I'm awake, I touch things, the fog is clearing . . . I'm cured . . . And now—just as he says (*pointing to Belcredi*)—yes, throw off the masquerade! Shake off the nightmare! Open the doors and windows!

Breathe in the air! Quick! Away! (*more calmly*) But where? For what? For everybody to point a furtive finger?—"There goes Henry IV!" And not as you see me now, but out in the world, arm in arm with you, my dear friends!

BELCREDI   It wouldn't be like that.

MATILDA   Who'd ever . . . ? It's unthinkable. It was an accident.

HENRY   They used to say I was cuckoo before I had the accident. (*to Belcredi*) You know that better than anyone— anybody who stuck up for me had you to deal with.

BELCREDI   Oh, come on, it was all in good heart.

HENRY   And there's my hair—look.

BELCREDI   But mine's going grey too.

HENRY   Yes, but there's a difference. I turned grey in here, as Henry IV. Can you understand what that means? I didn't realise!—I just noticed it one day, it was something of a shock, because I knew at once it wasn't just my hair. *I* was going grey, I was rotting away. I was done, I'd missed the feast.

BELCREDI   You weren't left abandoned . . .

HENRY   I know. They longed for me to get better. Even the one who was right behind me and jabbed my horse till the blood ran . . .

DI NOLLI   What?

HENRY   . . . jabbed it to make it rear up, till it threw me.

MATILDA   My God! It's the first I've heard of this!

HENRY   Was that in good heart, too, do you suppose?

MATILDA Who? Who was behind us?

HENRY What does it matter? It could as well have been any of those who went on to the banquet and would have saved me their meagre leftovers of sympathy, a few bones of contrition on the edge of their plates. Thank you very much!

So, Doctor—see if I'm not a first in the annals of lunacy! I decided to stay mad, finding everything I needed here for a completely new form of amusement, to live as a madman of sound mind. Maybe it was to get my own back on the paving stone that cracked my head. What I saw when I came round was desolation, bleak and empty, and I decided to deck it out in all the colours and splendour of that long-gone carnival day when you . . . oh, there you are, my lady . . . when you had your triumph . . . and to make everyone who came here continue—this time for my diversion—that celebrated masquerade which had been—for you if not for me—just the whim of a day . . . to make it last forever, not as make-believe now but as the real thing, the genuine mad article: the right clothes, the throne room, the four Privy Counsellors—all of them traitors, I gather—(*turning to them*) I'd like to know what you think you've gained by it? If I'm cured, you're out of a job. I must have been mad to confide in you. But now it's my turn. Guess what? They were thinking we could carry on this charade behind your backs!

Henry begins to laugh. The others, with the exception of Matilda, laugh too.

HENRY (*cont.*) Don't blame them. (*shaking his clothes*) We are what we wear. Look, this is an obvious, deliberate caricature of that other charade which is the life we live as puppets . . . so you have to forgive them, they don't realise it's only their frocks. (*to Belcredi*) You soon enter into the spirit of it. You start behaving as if you're in some tragedy, like this . . . (*He demonstrates.*) I'm cured, gentlemen, because I've woken up to my madness. So I'm calm. Your problem is you haven't woken up to yours, so you toss and turn your whole lives through.

BELCREDI   Oh, so in the end, we're the madmen, are we?

HENRY   Well, if you weren't crazy, would you have shown up here with her?

BELCREDI   I might if I thought you were crazy.

HENRY   And what about her?

BELCREDI   Ah, her . . . I don't know about her. She's hanging on to your every word, she seems quite entranced by your sane-as-a hatter emergence. (*to Matilda*) Since you're dressed for the part, Countess, why don't you join him?

MATILDA   Damn your insolence!

HENRY   Take no notice!—he can't help provoking me, though the Doctor warned him. (*to Belcredi*) Why should I care about what happened between us?—the part you played in my unlucky love . . . (*indicating Belcredi to Matilda*) . . . the part he now plays in your life! My life has been this one here. I wasn't there when you got old. Was that what you wanted to tell me, to show me, by dressing up, stooping to this—on doctor's orders? Nice one, Doctor. "Before" and "After," eh? But unfortunately for you, I'm not that crazy. I knew damn well he wasn't Henry IV. Because I'm Henry IV. I've been Henry IV for years . . . stuck behind my mask, while she's lived life and enjoyed herself for twenty years . . . and become—look at her there—someone I don't know anymore . . . because I know her like this . . . (*pointing at Frida and moving closer to* *her*) to me this will always be her. Now you look like little children ready to jump out of your skins. (*to Frida*) And you were frightened, weren't you, my sweet, by the game they tricked you into playing. How could you know it wasn't the game they thought it was? Oh, what a marvellous terror!—the dream that comes to life, never more alive than in you. You were only an image but they made you flesh . . . blood . . . breath. You're mine— mine!—mine by right!

Henry takes her in his arms, laughing insanely, while everybody shrieks in terror; but when they rush to pull Frida away from him he becomes menacing and shouts to his four Counsellors.

HENRY (*cont.*)   Hold them off! Hold them! I order you!

The four Counsellors, stunned, fascinated, automatically try to restrain Di Nolli, the Doctor, and Belcredi.

BELCREDI   Let go of her! Let go! You're no madman!

Henry takes Di Nolli's sword.

HENRY   Oh no? (*He runs Belcredi through.*) Are you sure?

Belcredi screams. Everyone rushes to Belcredi's aid, shouting in confusion.

DI NOLLI   Is it bad?

BERTOLD   Right in the guts!

DOCTOR   I warned you! Didn't I tell you?

FRIDA   Oh my God!

DI NOLLI   Frida, stay by me.

MATILDA   He's mad!—Mad!

DI NOLLI   Hold him down!

BELCREDI (*protesting fiercely*)   Oh no . . . there's nothing crazy about you! He's not mad! He isn't mad!

They take Belcredi, continuing to yell, out. Among the cries there is a more piercing one from Matilda, followed by silence.

Henry remains onstage, between Landolf, Harold, and Ordulf, with his eyes wide open, in astonishment.

HENRY   Now . . . yes . . . no two ways about it . . . Together again . . . Henry the Fourth, now and forever.

THE END